Healing Doves: Mental Health Poetry

Alexis R Tolkkinen

Ukiyoto Publishing

Dedication

"This book is dedicated to my wonderful mom, my uncle Rick who encouraged me on this journey, my dad and to my 7 boisterous siblings"

Contents

Alexis R Tolkkinen

Life

I keep trying to be
someone i'm not,
to write like a poet
 in love with the world
a writer on the verge of
madness
with a spark of genius
but
I am just sitting here
sipping on coffee
wishing i had a reason
 to move on.

Numb

I fell off the deep end
into nothingness
and for some reason
that great empty felt
better than feeling sad.

Alexis R Tolkkinen

A gardener never stops

I am on a journey to
replant the flowers of my spirit
even if that means growing
a few weeds in the process

Thunderstorm

We are under
 the same blue
sky
you and I
the only difference is
you no longer
appreciate it

constant beauty of the world
has numbed you to
it's awe
that's why an occasional thunderstorm
keeps one in perspective

for without the rain we'd
never grow to appreciate
the moments of silence,
our gardens
and sprouting flowers.

Alexis R Tolkkinen

Elderly

like a flower drawn to death
she shrivels
in the body she resides in

each wrinkle on her forehead, a ring of a cut down tree
for people to count.
each gray hair, the roots buried deep in the earth

there is such beauty in her branches
each blossom falling on soil, grass and graves

many decades of war, grief,
love and promises reside in her hunch
many stories settled in her brittle bones

many tears have fallen down that cheek
many smiles lit up her face

And most of all the gardens she tended, raised and watered
have grown up to call her a blessing
and that is the meaning of age.

Saved

You can't expect salvation
from a guy who doesn't
have the guts to tell you
that you're beautiful
on the days when you
 feel like you aren't.

You will need to
approach yourself
and offer a shield to your heart,
armor for the insults
and strength to leave
him when he no longer
gazes at you like art.

Alexis R Tolkkinen

Weight you carry

I don't expect you
to change immediately,
for the weight to
roll off your sleeves
but eventually you will
get strong enough
to carry it
and the pain will stop feeling
so deep.

Cliff

I don't judge you
for being "negative"
when the world trained you to
always be on edge
but i judge you
for pushing me
off.

Alexis R Tolkkinen

Fake Love

The way you fell
In love with her
when you promised me
us
reminds me that
fake love is
dangerous.

 if she makes you happy, I hope she doesn't treat you
like you treated me.

Mental fight

she was afraid of
her demons
even though they
Just needed love too.

Alexis R Tolkkinen

Ship

He is like

the ocean.

calm one day

a storm the next,

saying he'll stay

then he gets up and left

I tried to sail on his feelings

but i should've bought a ship

because his waves become monsters

and I needed to get away from his grip.

Listen

One is only called "broken"
by those not willing to listen.
Nobody is broken.
People are hurt.
There's a difference.

Alexis R Tolkkinen

The World is in pain

So often we assume nobody else

has ever gone through

the same thing

we do

but every single person

on this earth

has gone through something

So excruciatingly painful

they thought they'd never arrive safely at

the other side.

Comfort with pain

don't let sorrow

age in your mind

because it will

soon

seem normal

and you won't want to be

fine.

Alexis R Tolkkinen

Cosmos

She is beautiful

like the cosmos,

complex

yet so complete.

so why, he wondered, could she not see

the beauty in herself?

To stay alive

Some things just ring of poetry:

the grass on a warm windy day,

a dogs excited bark,

new friendships,

grandmothers cooking,

and a teachers passion.

Some things aren't like poetry at all:

death of a loved one,

wars,

gossip,

and tornados

but they are a reminder of why you need poetry. To stay alive.

Alexis R Tolkkinen

instagram

I fell into an algorithm
of assuming likes
meant my net value

simple

You say i write "simple short poetry",
but there is nothing simple about
a poem that reminds you
of a life you
have yet to live in the span
of a few words.

Alexis R Tolkkinen

Forget

I wish i could write a poem
to make you forget cruel words,
their taunts spin in air like smoke
waiting to damage and hurt.

I wish i could write a poem
to rid yourself from sorrow
but if i found a way to rid your pain today
how will you handle tomorrow?

If i write words sharp as knives
wouldn't we be like them?
words of hatred only come
from a hurt and damaged stem

My poems are for healing
but ultimately it's up to you
to pick their petals from the ground
and put them back with glue

when their words tumble back
remember to give them grace
for only a person hurt inside

taunts and shoves to win the race

winning is about loving

being the kindest in the room

for without love inside

we are simply as good as walking tombs

Alexis R Tolkkinen

feeding your monster

Stop giving them your jewels

We often let other
people's opinions
gain
power over us
like
diamonds

once we hand
them our gems
they produce
a laser
to cut us down.

We are not meant to have recycled hearts

but how else are we to rebuild ourselves

from their vile touch.

Alexis R Tolkkinen

el dorado

He thought
 her love was cheap
like fools gold
but could not see the
value resting in her soul

If you hold her but
do not value
her,
say you love her
but you do not

you are the reason she hid
who she was
you are the reason she
says her heart of gold is
lost.

heartbreak

I'd like to remember
a past heartbreak
forever

so when the day comes
when i truly love someone
and he loves me

and the cloudy skies
don't seem so dreary over the sea

we will laugh in the face
of what used to be
And i will say to heartbreak
"You never broke me"

Alexis R Tolkkinen

Stop trying to look for
"perfection"
in a person
instead look for who is worth
showing your imperfections to
In a world so photoshopped
and filtered,
In an age that is phony and fake.

She is so used to snakes

that she cannot recognize a king.

Alexis R Tolkkinen

love is everything

If you don't carry the same love towards her

as she carries for you

if you don't wish to rise up every morning

to talk with her,

walk with her,

and dance with her wild heart

next to yours

chances are

you never loved her at all.

words

She never deserved a guy
who only values her body
when there's so much more
beauty in her words.

Alexis R Tolkkinen

Violence

when the ocean

becomes violent

remember that

it was once calm too

but nobody says

"Move on. That was just one time "

when it's waves

almost drowned you

Pearls before Swine

The most beautiful hearts don't
show off their beauty
to everyone they see,
they wait for the right souls to
appreciate their light
like a boat looking out for a lighthouse
on the sea.

Light is never appreciated by those who love the dark.

Alexis R Tolkkinen

We were Something else

Our hearts are not punching bags

for poorly filtered emotions,

we are not streams

to be filled with dirt

and drained dry

for it turns out that we were

the flawless sea

with waves meant to reach the sunset sky.

Breaking

If being strong is about
never breaking
apart at times

let me be
"weak"

let me
 fall

let me
stutter

let my heart cleanse it's clutter
by revealing what I for so long kept
under

let me reveal
my thunder

let my wounds

Alexis R Tolkkinen

become power

let myself be considered "weak"
for feeling
alive
for my strength is in how i
i am unique

let me feel
alive
each minute by minute
each hour by hour

I am but human
weak and timid

for that is how i
bloom like a flower
with willingness to grow
and cry in the rainshower.

Butterfly

If you fall out of loving places though I once thought you'd stay there,

If i see my reflection as ugly

because you no longer smile and stare,

if i watch my heart grow dimmer

because you do not see

the ever changing heart i carry

then you do not deserve to witness

the butterfly emerging in me.

Alexis R Tolkkinen

Poets

I feel more alive among poets
for in their verses no one ever dies
they see the heart as a temple
and the soul eternal as starry skies

they weave many tales of battles
and many woes of men
but nothing can change a poets view
about the calling of the pen

they write of peaceful shores
heaven and of light
they do not quench their fire inside
though others say to "take fright!"

they live among the freesouls
hoping to bring others to peace
letter by letter, word by word
saying "with poems the heart will be free"

Every man is a poet
whether not he writes a rhyme,
Every woman is a poetess
even is she will not try,
every child is a writer
playing with stones and sticks
it's just a matter of listening
and building a palace of
poetic bricks.

Alexis R Tolkkinen

Rain

Do not stop the process of healing

just because it hurts

things are bound to get better

but first things will seem worse.

the pain inside will rise

like the rush of a tide

but before it settles far away

you will feel it deep inside.

the path to hope is rocky

to come up, one must trudge down

to find a smile in your being

you must first face what made you frown.

to live a life of joy is not to be rid of pain

but to say in the face of sadness

"I can dance in any rain"

Fires

We so often turn to fires

to hide parts of ourselves

that we deem undesirable

with our filters, with a lot of makeup, with our unhealthy dieting

by trying to bury

the beautiful gifts we contain

in our bodies

in our words and in our hearts

we pretend

that we are less real

to seem more smooth like gold

unrealizing that we

are the queens

and not the objects

in this story.

don't hide yourself.

Alexis R Tolkkinen

Asked for in me

I found you underneath the stars
dancing with the laughter I never had,
running with happiness inside your head
so how could I rip
the heart you healed?
how could I tell you to leave her,
the person you called home
in a million spaces.
how could i tell you to run back
when she is everything
you ever asked for in me?

Expectations

wishing

        to

fall in love

we abandoned

our own

        personal

routes

instead we took the backroads

only leading to others expectations

of

       us.

Alexis R Tolkkinen

She is perfect

not because he

said so

never because of him

but because she is

healed enough to believe

that the fire inside

would always be beautiful

no matter who sat by her flames.

I am sensitive but I am alive.

They laugh at me

for feeling more emotional

than them

as if there is an ugliness

to my sensitivity,

as if feeling alive

is equivalent

to sin.

Alexis R Tolkkinen

Danger

She was always taught the danger
of strangers,
to avoid backroads
and old hotels
but what she could never fathom
was the darkness in herself.

Tears are confetti
of the wasted youth,
decorating war wounds
with paint and booze.

Alexis R Tolkkinen

Diamonds are temporary

Over

being a diamond

In the palms of your hands

I'd rather be the dirt

so you can plant a garden

      in this

            godforsaken land

Bridges

If you tell me

that you are broken

I will not shame

the pieces of your heart

that were scorched in the flame

but i will tell you

how even

the strongest bridges

need mended at times

but through the mending

they are still

      whole.

Alexis R Tolkkinen

Fire

I

cant

see

beyond

the moments of

fire

ripping apart my soul and heart

ideas

and feelings

my soul often

doesn't know how to

shed it's skin and

go away

from the place it

was in

But i'll find out

how

since i'm a survivor

S

U

R

V

I

V

O

R

of the islands that drown lost sailors

mermaids that sing hearts to death

I will wander and find

my peace of mind

 and rest

Alexis R Tolkkinen

Catch more flies with honey

I will not fight
you
I will love you
softly
until
the feeling of
needing to
fight
fades.

Complete me

People always
say that a man will complete me

like wearing a diamond necklace or tiara
but
 i am a child of the wind and prairie

meant to roll in dirt
and run free

not to be imprisoned by the
expectations of jewelry
to make me shine.

instead i decorate myself with the wiles of nature,
completely immersed in it's pull

and its signs.

Alexis R Tolkkinen

City

If you read my thoughts
you'll see that i'm a person
who enjoys the city

surrounded by so many people
wrapped like books

with individual stories
so unique and tragic

and i'll never get to read them.

Moving on

I wrote a list of everything
I wished
to happen

and it never once
mentioned
you.

Alexis R Tolkkinen

Selfish

I
am
selfish
but in a good way

because if i wasn't
I don't think
I would have stayed

because we need a little bit
of selfishness to
get us through the day

"Please Paint"

Never give pain a place to nest in your beating heart
Instead let it
 work through you

Like art
Because

You are the artist
And every tear,
Every laugh,
Every choice is your paint.

Please paint yourself kindly.

Alexis R Tolkkinen

"Self Betrayal"

As women
We know the feeling
Of self betrayal

We tell ourselves
We aren't beautiful enough because
A man can't appreciate

Our smiles

Our strength

Our sacred love

And it's about time that we've said
"Enough!" to being a man's playground

Because we've always been beautiful

But they didn't have the strength to
see it.

"I Will not Swim"

I will not just

Swim

Through my existence

I will dive and make a splash

So loud that

The earth hears my strength.

Alexis R Tolkkinen

"Feel it"

Every once in a while sadness
Will peak from behind the curtains
And turn off the lights
But perhaps that's how
The shadows fade from my mind.

Maybe I have to feel it to get rid of it?

About the Author

Alexis Tolkkinen lives in Ohio on a farm with 7 younger siblings. She is going to college for an English degree.